The Gospel According to Sidney:

The Reversed Version

By:
T. Douglas Butters

PublishAmerica
Baltimore

© 2005 by T. Douglas Butters.
All rights reserved. No part of this book may be reproduced, stored in a retrieval system or transmitted in any form or by any means without the prior written permission of the publishers, except by a reviewer who may quote brief passages in a review to be printed in a newspaper, magazine or journal.

At the specific preference of the author, PublishAmerica allowed this work to remain exactly as the author intended, verbatim, without editorial input.

First printing

ISBN: 1-4137-8591-3
PUBLISHED BY PUBLISHAMERICA, LLLP
www.publishamerica.com
Baltimore

Printed in the United States of America

Dedication

This book of poems is dedicated to my wife, Pamela Kaye.
Pam has stood beside me for 36 years.
I dedicate this book to my daughters and their husbands:
Tonia and Mike Snider, Terra and John Qsler and
Tabitha and Thomas Qualls.
As well, I dedicate this book to our parents,
Darrel and Marcia Butters
and Richard and Mary Tittle Their prayerful, loving
presence has been a blessing to me.

Mary Ann
God bless you!
I am honored by your
loving kindness. It's good
to be in the same family
Terry
Douglas Butters

Acknowledgments:

*I want to thank my friend, Jim Peter
for all his help with my computer.
He enabled me to make the best of a old system.*

*I want to thank my mother, Marcia Butters
for her help with editing.*

*I want to thank Scott's Studio
for the great pictures.*

*I have to thank the people I served as Pastor in
Flint during the early years, as Sidney developed.
The folks at First Church of the Brethren,
were with me, in so many ways.*

*Finally, I want to thank my good friend, Rev. John Gruntham
for listening with an open mind and heart, as I
shared with him my dreams for Sidney.*

*My thanks to James E. VanAllen Jr. for drawing
Sidney for me.*

Contents

7	The Trophy	93	The Election
10	The Plan	96	The Canoe
13	The Creatures	99	The Sale
14	SIDNEY	102	The Work Day
16	The Sermon:	105	The Membership Board
19	The Program	108	The Fellowship Committee
22	The List	111	The Neighbor
25	The Line	114	The Evaluation
28	The Egg Hunt	117	The revival
31	The Painting	120	The Helper
34	The Image	123	The Cousin
37	The Plaque	126	The Ad
40	The Pin	129	The Youth Pastor
43	The Excuse	132	The Golfers
46	The Glitter	135	The Bus
49	The Candy Bar	138	The Christmas List
52	The Women	141	The Graveyard
55	The New Pastor	144	The Invitation
58	The Budget	147	The Guests
61	The Confrontation	150	The Diagnosis
64	The Congressman	153	The Candidate
67	The Picket Line	156	The Yard
69	The Task Force	159	The Homeless
72	The Bank Line	162	The Poultry Nest
75	The Book Store	165	The Garden
78	The Stop Sign	168	The Leak
81	The Flat Tire	171	The Suitcase
84	The Planning Board	174	The Suit
87	The Mall	177	The Kit
90	The Traffic Stop	180	The Bible

The Trophy

Hello, Pastor, this is Sid.
I know why you called this man.
You want me to represent our church.
Well, I believe I can.

I've thought long and hard on this,
and I'm afraid, I really fear
There's no one here as good as me
To be "Christian of the Year".

Just look at my credentials,
Out front where all can see.
There's no one better suited
For this honor than good ol' me.

And so, you will need reasons
Which I can, of course, provide.
I'm not ashamed of who I am;
I've nothing now to hide.

In your mind's eye, can you see
The third pew from the rear?
My family has sat there
Since the church was first built here.

If I were not so pious,
I'd most likely raise a fuss
To name the church after me,
Or, at least, to name our bus.

Then, of course, there is my ministry
Of always helping out.
Why, just last week, Elrod Groom
Was suffering with the gout.

There he stood, could barely walk;
So, I offered him a place.
It's good that our club's golf carts
Are built with an extra space.

Oh, Pastor, I could go on and on,
But you know that I am right.
Just tell me where I am to go,
And I'll be there that night.

Oh, I see, but of course,
That night will be okay.
Can the family come along,
And will they have to pay?

THE LORD SPEAKS:
Say, Sid, about the contest,
That trophy sure looks great.
Setting up there on your mantle;
Ten pounds must be its weight.

Sidney, you were speechless,
When the M. C. announced the name,
Your wife, was selected,
At least, the last name is the same.

The Plan

Hello, Pastor. This is Sidney.
I've taken your plan to heart.
And when it's printed up,
I'm ready, then, to start.

I think that resolutions
Are important to us all.
So, the ones I select,
Will be placed upon my wall.

My resolutions for this year,
Are for my spirit's need.
I must make sure I'm living right,
So I'm planting now new seed.

If I can do these things,
I'll know I'm on my way
To earning me a special spot
In the Land of Eternal Day.

First of all, there's praying,
At least six times a day;
So, I've bought a little book
That shows for me the way.

You've got to have an attitude
In position, speech, and tone.
So, I must now get busy,
And my prayerful technique hone.

Then, there's going to church.
Attending without fail,
I'm told, will really guarantee,
Into heaven, I will sail.

So, I'm going every Sunday,
Except when I'm away.
Now, all that's left is my tithe
And the amount I will pay.

I'll set aside a goodly sum,
Each one, a small bill,
So there'll be lots to give
When I dump it in the till.

Well, there it is, my ticket
To that Heavenly Portal bright.
Now, I'll keep these commitments
With all my earthly might.

THE LORD SPEAKS:

Well, Sid, that is all and good,
But it's not the place to start.
I need to see you changing things,
First, within your heart.

You must, you see, be born again,
Then all the rest will come.
Starting out the way you are
Leaves your spirit kind of numb.

The Creatures

Hello, Pastor. I need your help.
I'm confused by what I've read.
I've started reading *Ezekiel*,
And I'm messed up in my head.

It says Ezekiel saw a windstorm
With a lot of flashing light,
And in the fire, you won't believe,
Was really quite a sight.

He writes of four creatures
With legs just like a calf.
These glowed like burnished bronze,
And, Pastor, that's just half.

Each thing had four faces,
An eagle, a lion, an ox, and a man.
Well, Pastor, that settled it.
So, here will be my plan.

I'm going to take my Saturdays,
Rewriting all the book.
Can you come over soon
And take a careful look?

I'm cutting out all the part
That are hard to understand.
What will be left, I am sure,
Will be cherished throughout the land.

THE LORD SPEAKS:

Say, Sid, before the Reverend comes,
I'll share a thought or two.
It seems you've taken liberty,
In more places than a few.

What about My man Jonah?

SIDNEY:

I struggled with that a bit,
But Lord, he had to go.
Staying alive inside a fish
Is impossible, You know.

THE LORD SPEAKS:

Oh, and where is the lions' den
Where Daniel spent the night?
Remember, you had to cut it out,
Because it gives children quite a fright.

And, what about the miracles
Folks saw my Son perform?
Do you think the supernatural,
In life is not the norm?

Well, you've done a real good job,
If you do say so yourself.
But, if I were you, I'd put your book
Up on a real high shelf.

It's time for folks to realize,
My Word comes all intact.
And, Sid, old boy, you'd best learn
The Bible's not talk, but fact.

The Sermon:

Honey, that sermon moved me.
We've got to take more time,
Doing the really religious things
That will help our spiritual climb.

Let's review our schedule
When together we all are,
Not counting, of course, the many times
We're traveling in our car.

There are two times in the day
When we can meet during the week,
And each of them, leaves a lot,
Of desires for us to seek.

Six to seven at the dawn
And six to seven at night
But, getting up or missing the news,
For none of us is right.

Saturday seems to have lots of time,
Except from nine 'til ten.
Wriffel the Wonderful Wanderer
Comes on with his band of men.

I've watched Wriffel many years,
And I've learned from his show.
It was from him I found out,
That when it's cold, rain turns to snow.

Let's not forget, the afternoons
Are reserved for the ball game,
And if we missed the pre-game show,
It wouldn't be the same.

Now, we're down to Sunday.
With church, there's no time then.
So, let's ask the Pastor.
Maybe, he can tell us when.

THE PASTOR:
Sidney, thanks for asking.
My sermon spoke to me, too.
The hours I have after ministry time,
For me, as well, are few.

The answer God has shown me,
In our spare time can be found.
And, it's certainly not as easy
As I made it all to sound.

THE LORD SPEAKS:

Sid, your Pastor's quite a guy
To confess like that to you;
And the lesson he has learned
Is one that is not new.

Sid, what can you give up
To make some time for Me?
Could it be Saturday, at nine,
You'll find an hour that's free.

The Program

It's not too often that I complain
When things are not going right.
But, Pastor, your new program
Has kept me up at night.

This plan to take folks at their word,
And hold them to the line,
Has hurt a lot of feelings.
But, of course, it's not hurt mine.

Why, talking just the other day
With dear old Itema Store,
She said she's not too happy
And may walk out the door.

Then I talked to Hileel Perk;
He expressed much the same.
"It will not work." he told me,
So he won't play the game.

I, have thought it through,
And, of course, will give it a try,
But I'm afraid the other folks
Would just as soon let it die.

I've polled the Board as a result;
They think that it will work.
But looking closely as they spoke,
I detected, I think, a smirk.

Most folks aren't like you and me;
You cannot take their word.
And, as a matter of fact,
You won't believe what I just heard.

The former Chairman of the Board,
Good old Tillmore Krunk,
Known as a great abstainer,
Just last night was seen drunk.

Now, of course, this is a rumor,
And it may not, after all, be true,
But I have doubts of Tillmore;
This rumor is not new.

Pastor, what this really says,
Is you'd best withdraw your plan.
Folks will not keep their word;
I just don't think they can.

THE LORD SPEAKS:

Well, Sid, why not come out and say it.
You don't like it, too.
You may have fooled the pastor,
But, I see right through you!

You cannot keep your word at all,
No matter what you say.
If you'd just stop your little lies,
I could really make your day.

The List

The Pastor has asked we make a list,
Of Christmas gift wishes we could abort.
I'm to write down what I'd like to get
If money was running short.

It's hard to think it happening,
Getting gifts…just a few,
But I suppose it's possible,
So I'll hurry and get this through.

If I had just three gifts
That I could ever get,
The first thing I really need
Is awfully large and wet.

Raoul's Ready-Made Hot Tubs
Has got a hot tub special buy,
To take away my stress,
With temperatures from Boil to Fry.

The second gift I really need,
To some may seem a toy,
But if I get this item,
It would bring me lots of joy.

Jerome Jasper's Jumping Gym
Is equipped with this and that,
And if I use it faithfully,
I'll get rid of all this fat.

If I could only have one more,
It really ought to be
A simple little instrument
That will help me the heavens see.

Sylvester Starbright's Stellar Scope
Will bring to earth the sky.
For when I see a shooting star,
I breathe an awestruck sigh.

Yes, Pastor, with just these three,
I'll be pleased as punch;
And, as you well can see,
I've not asked for a bunch.

I'm known as a simple man.
My praises, I don't sing.
Say, is it too late to change
Number three to a diamond ring?

THE LORD SPEAKS:

I like your list, Simple Sid,
But you've misread your pastor's mind.
The gifts he asked you of
Are for other folks to find.

I seems the most important thing
Is "Get the most, not give."
And if this attitude keeps its course,
The Christmas Spirit will not live.

The Line

Oh, Pastor, I'm so glad you came
To supper here tonight,
And while we wait for the meal,
I'll show you quite a sight.

As you well know, my family
Has held the deacon post,
From the beginning of our church,
And, as well, contributed the most.

Well, next week is the election,
And it's time for me to run;
And when I am elected deacon,
The job, I will get done.

Why, just look at these pictures,
Three generations back.
As I tell you their story,
You'll see nothing that I lack.

My father, Sidney Number three,
Served as deacon 'til this year.
He never ever backed away
From a problem out of fear.

His father, Sidney Number Two,
Knew always what to say;
And because he spoke right out,
He always got his way.

Now, there is Sidney Number One,
My esteemed great-grand pop.
He served the church faithfully;
No one could make him stop.

Without a doubt, Sidney One
By himself, led the way
To what our church has become
As we stand here today.

So, Pastor, as you can see,
The deacon's job is mine.
You might as well appoint me,
For I will do just fine.

I know that Birchwood Grassfump
Hoped this year he would win
The job as our next deacon,
But we've got to put me in.

THE LORD SPEAKS:

Excuse Me, Sidney Next-in-line,
Pride is knocking at your door;
And for the sake of the church,
Please step down, I implore.

Whenever someone thinks he owns
A position on the Board,
The devil's won a victory,
Then, he rules, not the Lord.

The Egg Hunt

Pastor, can I buy you breakfast,
Or, will a cup of coffee do?
Regular or decaffeinated,
How about cream and sugar, too?

Well, I'd best get to the point.
There's a rumor that I've heard,
And, Pastor, I must tell you,
My heart is deeply stirred.

Tomorrow will be Easter,
And yet you've failed to plan
To celebrate the holiday,
So tell me if you can.

How will we make it special
For all who come to church?
I'd hate to think that visitors
Will be left out in the lurch.

PASTOR:
Well, Sid, I'm glad you asked,
And I don't know who's to blame,
But, from the mailing list,
Someone dropped your name.

Our Easter celebration,
Is planned out to a "T".
Just listen now, and I'll tell you
About all that you will see.

Our choir has a Cantata
That will thrill the soul,
But that's not all we do;
They're just part of the whole.

The message I've been working on
Will stir folks to repent,
And as I share the Word of God,
Folks will know it's heaven-sent.

Pastor, that's all well and good,
But you've missed, I feel, the key.
There's more of us, I am sure,
That feel a lot like me.

You've got to do it for the kids,
So please don't make me beg.
We cannot celebrate Easter
Without hunting for an egg.

THE LORD SPEAKS:

Sid, save me a peanut butter egg,
I love them, yes, I do.
And so to use my time more wisely,
I'll eat it when the sermon's through.

I hope you folks won't get bored
When my story he will share.
I sure don't want to cheat the hunt,
So he'll make it quick up there.

The Painting

Pastor, I just read a book
By a man from the Irkestrain.
His name is Nugbumavich,
And he doesn't have a brain.

He smuggles Bibles to his land,
And sneaks them over the line.
If he's not very careful,
He'll be a prisoner, with a hefty fine.

I think getting carried away
Causes more problems than it's worth.
Take for instance, a case in point,
Old Mike DeAngelo Perth.

He was a member years ago,
He believed that painting was his call.
Well, he had a dream one Christmas Eve,
And that was his downfall.

He dreamed that he painted
The Wise men on the search,
And God told him to paint one
In town at every single church.

He believed that it symbolized
The searching sinner's life,
And that the painting's message,
Could help free them from their strife.

Now, all ten churches got theirs
By the next Christmas Eve,
And him, being awfully shy,
He'd carry it inside, then leave.

But, we were not so lucky.
For us he'd start the task
Of painting our dining hall ceiling.
Though for it we did not ask.

Now, I'll admit it was good,
But, Pastor, believe you me,
Camels crossing desert sand
At every dinner we would see!

Yes, Mike lay on his back
And painted for a year.
That he'd not stop for anything,
He made very, very clear.

We planned a party to celebrate,
By raising to him a cup.
Then he died in a week or so,
And we covered the painting up.

So, Pastor, I really think
Such fervor is a waste.
Standing up when others want to sit,
To me, is just bad taste.

THE LORD SPEAKS:

The painting, it was beautiful,
But the congregants, they were not.
Especially your decision,
To scrape and repaint it on the spot.

By the way, in a year or so,
Old Mike will be a artist of great renown,
And a collector would have offered millions,
If you could have taken the ceiling down.

The Image

Pastor, I must really talk to you.
I know you're new in town,
And the last thing I want is...
See, the city father's frown.

You see, there is an image
That all of our pastors fit,
And you're not living up to code,
So on the sidelines you must sit.

Every pastor in our town
Belongs to the Richwell Club.
They've got the finest golf course
And a redwood board hot tub.

The membership is provided by
The downtown Merchant's League,
Of which, I am vice-president,
Serving under Slopwell Cleeg.

Every pastor in our town
Shops in Slipshod;s Silk & Satin Shop.
He has the finest suits anywhere,
And someday, you should stop.

Slipshod's suits are well-made,
And, of course, they're not cheap,
But based on what we pay you,
His price should not seem steep.

Every pastor in our town
Drives a big Stretch LaVille,
Provided by Crankshaft Grease.
You'll like him, yes, you will.

He sells more high dollar cars
Than any dealer in the state.
So, head on down and pick one out.
There is no need to wait.

Yes, Pastor, do not hesitate,
For image is the key
To seeing the church live out
All that it can be.

No one can doubt our great wealth
When they see you suited in the car,
And folks will want to be a part;
They will come from near and far.

THE LORD SPEAKS:

Sidney, I was thinking.
What should the image be
Of a man or woman set apart
To preach about what is free?

Can the message of salvation
Really touch a heart,
When the pastor is more concerned
When his Stretch LaVille won't start?

The Plaque

Pastor, I've thought it through carefully,
And with great gratitude, I volunteer.
But, before I leave the church house,
Let me make one thing clear.

I'm not one to make a fuss
About the work I do,
So a simple plaque out in the foyer,
Will suffice when I am through.

I've been gathering all I need
For this mission from the Board.
I love it when there's a need
To bravely serve the Lord.

I've memorized sixty-four
Heart-rending true-life tales,
That are designed to motivate
Even bullies to sobs and wails.

I've a tract for every argument
Known to every sinful man.
You know, I think I will succeed.
At least, I think I can.

You'd better call out the warriors
To surround me with lots of prayer.
I suggest ten per hour
To let God know they care.

I'm carrying a new witnessing tool.
It's called the *Slim Line Sword*.
There's lots of verses to choose from
To point folks to the Lord.

It fits into a comb case
Which I keep in my suit.
It has a picture of strong Samson;
With long hair he looks cute.

Well, here goes, Sidney.
Just step up and speak your mind.
"Good afternoon, Mr. Farquar.
A few minutes can you find?

I'm from the church next door,
And I've got for you a plan.
You can't go on for long like this,
Even though you think you can."

THE LORD SPEAKS:

Sidney, you're a genius!
None can succeed like you.
I listened as you laid it out;
He was moved when you were through.

Oh, by the way, he's out there now
Moving his pick-up truck.
He'll not park on the church lot again
When his dirt driveway turns to muck.

The Pin

Pastor, thank you for this pin.
It goes in a special place.
I've got a drawer in my desk
That's got a lot of space.

Why not wear this pin?
Well, it's got our church's name
All around the edge,
And I don't play this witnessing game.

That's not to say I have no faith,
For you know that isn't true.
The name-plate on our family pew
Is well-worn, not new.

The *Reserved* sign at our parking space
Has my name in black,
And anyone can see it,
If they drive out back.

Once each year I take the Board
Downtown for a lunch;
They can get all they want
At the *Snack and Lunch*.

Then I take them to my store
On a shopping spree
To buy supplies for the church,
The first twenty bucks on me.

A quick look at the record book
Will speak for itself.
My attendance and our offering charts
Take up one whole shelf.

I've held every office in the church,
Except in the Ladies Aid.
I suggest my record shows
My dues have well been paid.

So, Pastor, it's very clear.
At least, it is to me.
My faithfulness to the church
Is there for all to see.

But, Pastor, you have spoken to me,
So yes, I'll wear this little pin.
I'll get out my Sunday suit,
And to its lapel, I'll stick it in.

THE LORD SPEAKS:

Sid, in church, you are doing well.
But, outside, not so good.
There is no place outside the church,
For your secret Christian hood.

You cannot plant your seed in the church;
In there it will not grow.
So wear the pin every day,
Then your faith in God will show.

The Excuse

Pastor, you want me go where?
To Mexico with a team?
Where we will build a church?
This must be a bad dream!

You heard me right. I said "bad dream".
I've a problem. That's for sure,
And although I'm usually first to help,
Staying home is my only cure.

First of all, there is my time.
For three weeks, I can't go.
I've far too much to do right here,
That fact you should well know.

As chairman of the Christmas Creche,
More time I must devote.
I cannot find a camel,
And I only have one goat.

Five hundred bucks for three weeks
Is something I've not got,
For I'm taking Honey and the kids
To a resort, and cheap it's not!

We need a vacation,
And its cost will be real great;
So, a trip to Mexico
Will simply have to wait.

Last, there is my problem
Of getting too much sun.
As you well know, a sunburn
Never is much fun.

Besides in Old Mexico
The water is no good,
So I'd be better off to stay at home,
I really think I should.

Why not ask Gilthorp Schmock?
He loves to work in dirt,
And if he gets lost in Mexico,
It really wouldn't hurt.

Gilthorp loves the poor folks,
And in our church, there's none.
Say, how about a coffee,
Now that we've got that done?

THE LORD SPEAKS:

Sid, I really wanted you to go,
To learn to give not take.
But, ever even asking you
Was somehow a big mistake.

I don't think you understand,
Or ever will really see
That when you help other folks,
You're really helping Me.

The Glitter

Pastor, you won't believe where I've been!
Last Sunday when out of town,
I visited a great big church
That's shaped like a crown.

All That Really Matters Is Love
Is the name it goes by.
And, Pastor, what I saw there
Would make a rich man cry.

We've failed the Lord terribly
With our church the way it is.
The problem that we have
Is that we have no whiz.

I saw a church that's alive
With people filled with joy.
I'll tell you all about it.
Are you ready for this, Old Boy?

The fifteen spires of the church
Blink with colored lights.
You should have seen the crowd.
It's one of the town's best sights.

The church is in a circle
With the spires all spaced around,
And bells are ringing from each one;
You can't believe the sound.

A snack bar's in the foyer;
They sell the food at cost.
It wouldn't do, the pastor said,
To go and cheat the lost.

Everyone sits in bucket seats,
Complete with a foot rest.
The seats are covered in leather;
They only have the best

They have a fifty foot video screen
For viewing live TV;
For every show they have on,
Every seat is free.

Behind the pulpit, center stage,
Is a pool Olympic size.
It's for mass baptism;
At least, I would surmise.

The pastor came strolling down the aisle,
Dressed in sparkling white,
In a suit of Spandex
That fit him very tight.

Everyone reached to touch his hem;
With each touch he gave a smile.
As he walked he turned around,
Arms extended all the while.

He preached of love and what it does
And the success that it can bring.
He turned and called to the choir;
You should have heard them sing.

Pastor, I was impressed!
They put on a great show.
There's no doubt in my mind
Why they grow and grow.

THE LORD SPEAKS:

So, Sid, you met Reverend Love
And sat in his bucket seat,
But while you sat and watched the show,
With you I did not meet.

The glitter, flash, and spectacle
Impressed me not a bit.
The only light I care about
Is the one inside that's lit.

The Candy Bar

Pastor, you've got to help me!
I've got to break the grip
That chocolate has on my life
Before we take our trip.

We're going South again,
And Candy Land we'll pass through.
You, of course, know what is wrong;
My sweet tooth is not new.

The last time we went through there,
I purposed in my heart
That when it came to eating candy,
I simply would not start.

Well, we pulled into Candy Land,
And, Pastor, wouldn't you know?
There was a giant candy bar'
Hanging there all aglow.

I tried not to look at it,
And although it was not real,
Deep within my taste buds,
A yearning I could feel.

To quench my thirst for chocolate,
I bought just a bit.
Little did I realize
I'd have a chocolate fit.

Soon I was running down the street,
Rushing from shop to shop.
Stuffing candy into my mouth,
I simply could not stop.

At last I bought a ten pound box,
With all kinds of treats to pick.
I ate them all that evening,
And promptly, I got sick.

So you see, dear Pastor,
You must help me, Sir, and quick.
I think a little prayer or two
Will surely do the trick.

Just ask God to tell me when
I've eaten to my fill,
For I can't stop on my own;
I haven't got the will.

THE LORD SPEAKS

Oh, Sid, your pastor spoke to me
About your little need.
But I can't do a thing for you
While you, your habit feed.

The only way out for you
Is chocolate never touch.
For if you keep on tasting it,
I really can't do much.

The Women

Pastor, you've got to watch this tape!
I recorded it just last night.
Although at first, it sounded strange,
Now I think he's right

He's chairman of a group called W. O. O. L.
Which means *Women Overrunning Our Land.*
And here are the principles
On which all men should stand.

First, they want all women
To be kept at home.
"It's a fact," he told us,
"Outside, they're apt to roam."

He said, "They're just like cattle,
And can't handle all life's change.
They're better kept in a corral,
Just cooking on the range."

The second group they oppose
Is women who want to work;
For when they're in an office,
Their home duties they will shirk.

"It is a crime," he told us,
"And it's got to stop!
Besides, it's true that women
Would rather like to shop."

The third group they oppose
Is the woman athlete.
The last thing a man needs
Is a woman jogger on the street.

He said to take their gym shoes
And replace them with a broom;
Most can always start a sweat
By sweeping out a room.

"Somehow, we've got to get control,"
Dr. Farfleet finally said,
"Before the rights of women
Result in a swelled head."

I'm going to go out on a limb
And invite Farfleet here,
For you've been duped by women,
Dear Pastor, I do fear.

THE LORD SPEAKS:

*Say Sid, I saw Dr. Farfleet.
I don't think that he can come,
His wife got called out of town,
And this will surprise you some.*

*She's the President of a college,
And to a Conference she must go.
So, the good Dr. Farfleet,
Must watch the kids, you know.*

The New Pastor

Well , it's time to choose a pastor,
And you've picked out the right man
To select all our guidelines.
I can do it, yes, I can!

We need a man to lead us
Who will point us to the right,
So to keep us all focused,
We'll keep these points in sight

A pastor must be healthy,
So we look first for his youth.
He must have lots of energy
To preach to us the truth.

Besides, if he is young,
He'll be there when we call,
To save Widow Creepwell's kitty,
So from the rooftop it won't fall.

Our pastor must be brilliant.
He needs an education grand
From the finest institution
To be found in our land.

I think, at least, a P. H. D.
In Psychology is a must,
For having just a Masters
Would make his counsel hard to trust.

The final thing that we need
Is powerful preaching skill.
His pulpit time must wow us,
So our spirits they will thrill.

Yes, a real pulpit pounder
With a booming voice so great,
That we will tremble in our seats
As we ponder each our fate.

I emphasize again, we need a man
Who is healthy, young, and smart,
And, of course, an eloquent speaker
Is exactly where we start.

When we find the right man,
We'll be well on our way,
So let's bring in the first man
And hear what he has to say.

THE LORD SPEAKS:

Do you remember, Sidney,
What folks called My boy?
They often called Him Rabbi,
For His teaching brought them joy.

I don't recall you mentioning
Bible teaching on your list;
So, I suppose in your excitement,
That one, you simply missed.

The Budget

You know, Pastor, we've a problem.
You've gone too far this time.
The church will not support their going;
We'll not raise one dime.

There's no use in doing it,
No matter how we try.
We can't support their ministry,
And I'll tell you why.

First, our numbers are but few.
That proves to me one thing.
We've got to build ourselves up
Before mission bells will ring.

We've got to give our message
Better here at home,
Before we pay for others
Through Africa to roam.

Our budget is not working;
We've not a cent to spare.
I've talked to our treasurer;
The money's just not there.

We've trimmed our budget to the bone,
Line by line by page.
The only other place to turn
Is cutting back your wage.

Finally, I often wonder
If Africans really care,
Or would they rather have us
Stay far away from there?

I think their pagan ways
Will always just be that,
So why not keep out of there;
Then, our witness won't fall flat.

Well, that settles that!
Now, on to Item Two.
If we can just resolve this thing,
Our meeting can be through.

Our sanctuary is bulging;
We can't get anymore in,
So the million dollar building
Will help more folks to win.

THE LORD SPEAKS:

Hold it! Am I hearing things?
Is there something that I missed?
I thought there were a few of you
All with an empty fist.

You've faith enough to build a church,
When millions are at stake,
But sending folks to Africa
Is a chance you cannot take.

The Confrontation

Well, I don't know, Pastor,
I'll have to think this through.
Can I call you right back,
Say, in an hour or two?

Hello, Pastor. Well, I'm your man.
I'll check that new club out.
If it's as bad as you think,
You can be sure I'll shout.

Boy, it sure is dark inside,
And the music is so loud.
Just look at all these folks;
They sure are not my crowd!

Yes, I'd like a quiet spot
Somewhere near the back.
I'll also have a diet pop
And some French fries for a snack.

Let's see, Who's on the show bill?
It's Little Lulu Larue.
I've not heard of her before,
So her act must be new.

Why, look at her standing there
In a dress from head to toe.
If she can sing like she looks,
This will be one great show.

Miss, please bring by my check,
I've really got to go.
No, everything was just fine,
And that's really quite a show.

Please give my thanks to Lulu.
Yes, I know that she's not through;
But I'm seeing far too much of her,
For she's wearing just one shoe.

Well, I'm back home, Pastor,
And that was quite a shock;
But, before we protest too much,
Let's carefully take stock.

We'd better leave them alone,
Or trouble we will find.
We'll bite off more than we can chew
By messing with their kind.

THE LORD SPEAKS:

So, Sid, you'd just sit by
And let Lulu do her thing?
I thought you had some principles,
And to them you would cling.

When are you ever going to learn
That you need not live in fear?
You need to stand up to what is wrong.
That's why I put you here!

The Congressman

Pastor, you have touched a nerve.
At that meeting, I'll be there.
Unless we all take a stand,
No one will know we care.

You've asked that I support the right
Of hiring all Christian staff
For the school in our church,
By speaking on our behalf.

I'll call my District House Member
And take him out to lunch.
Fillpert and I were real close;
We ran in the same bunch.

He'll listen to what I say;
I'll make him understand.
If we don't defeat this bill,
We'll all lose in our land.

Fillpert, thanks for meeting me.
I've a lot on my mind.
There's a bill in Congress
That's causing me a bind.

But, before I speak of it,
Tell me what's new with you.
What bills have great importance?
There must be quite a few.

So, you're co-sponsoring a bill
To eliminate bias from every shop,
And when it passes through the House,
To the Senate it will hop.

You say we have no right to discriminate
For any reason anymore,
And when this bill passes through,
We'll be the land of the open door.

Fillpert, you'll not believe this.
My concern is just like yours.
I, too, am disturbed by what you call
The closing of the doors.

Do what you can to make it fair
Is all I really ask,
And whatever you do, my dear friend,
Don't stop 'til you finish the task.

Pastor, I told him how I felt,
But it didn't do much good.
He told me, too, how he felt,
How if he could he would.

I think it best to write a note
To our President.
It's only there, I'm afraid,
Our letters should be sent.

THE LORD SPEAKS:

Well, Sid old boy you did it,
You dropped the ball again!
You shared the who and what,
But not the why and when.

Convictions are not shared haphazardly.
And while there is no need to shout,
There will be times when we must,
Without fear, speak right out.

The Picket Line

Pastor, thanks for asking me.
It's time we take a stand
Against the pornographic smut
That's filling up our land.

Why, all across America,
There's a store in every town.
It's time we put ourselves to work
To shut those places down.

Well, I don't know. A picket line?
Do you think we ought to try?
There's got to be some other way
To make those smut kings cry.

How about a survey of the town
To find out how they feel?
Then we'll know beyond a doubt
If this problem's real.

Well, OK, I'll try to come.
When do you want me there?
That's not good. How about next week?
I'll have some time to spare.

Say, how about the graveyard shift?
That's probably hard to fill,
And even though it's cold at night,
I hardly ever chill.

THE PASTOR SPEAKS:
The problem, Sid, is you're afraid
To stand out from the crowd.

It's time you learned the Lord above
Wants us to speak out loud.

Oh, sure, we need those quiet times
When to God alone we speak,
But never do we find a time
When Christians can be weak.

Now's your chance to leave your mark
On a world that's bound in sin.
Instead of sneaking in the night,
In daylight march right in.

You need not fear what others think,
Or how on you they look;
You're simply doing what you're told
By Jesus in the Book.

It's time we set aside our fear
And stand for what is right.
Remember, Sid, the Lord in heaven
Is keeping us in sight.

He's looking for believers now
To carry out His plan
To free the world from Satan's power,
And you, Sid, are His man.

The Task Force

As chairman of this task force,
Chosen from the city's best,
We've got to do a good job.
We can't let down the rest.

We're to select the Social Problems,
Our city must address;
Then send them to the Council
And they'll give them to the Press.

Number One has got to be the schools.
Their failure, we must treat;
For only as they improve,
Good standards do they meet.

One major step that we can take
To best upgrade our school
Is to rip out the old tennis courts
And put in an Olympic pool.

The second problem that we face
We see on every street.
The solution, as I see it,
Will come as we hire feet.

The snow on our sidewalks
Stays there much too long.
Let's hire lots of scrapers,
With muscles big and strong.

The third problem that we see,
Which is, as well, the last,
Has to do with housing
Created in the past.

Far too many homes in town,
We can count them by the score,
Have just one tiny bathroom;
They all need to have one more..

I sure appreciate your help today
To make a better town.
As we make these changes,
Newcomers will not frown.

Well, men, our task is done.
Let's do lunch at the club,
And then gather at the first tee,
And our golf balls scrub.

THE LORD SPEAKS:

I think you missed your calling, Sid.
A politician, you should be.
You look right past the issues,
And good times, are all you see

Your kids are failing right and left;
The homeless line the street.
Too many kids in rental homes
Sleep with roaches at their feet.

The Bank Line

Don't even ask why I'm late!
I'm so mad, I can't see straight!
At the bank this afternoon
I had to stand and wait.

Why is it that it's always me
Who's asked to step aside.
I've got rights like everyone,
Yet over me folks ride.

Honey, there I was, stepping up
To the teller with my check,
When the manager stepped behind
And tapped me on the neck.

"Sir, could you let this lady in,"
He asked me with a frown.
"Her six kids are running out in front,
And a car might run them down."

She had so many things to do,
I stepped right out of line,
And walked two rows down
To enter the express line.

The man who stood in front of me
Ignored me when I spoke;
He wouldn't even turn around.
I almost gave to him a poke.

When he stepped up to the booth,
My heart began to sing.
The teller, then, asked for help.
The man couldn't hear a thing.

Then began a little game
Of notes passed to and fro.
In desperation I looked around
For another place to go.

Just past the lady with the kids,
I saw a teller open up.
I got in line just behind
A boy with a Collie pup.

The dog soon began to squirm,
And the boy set it on the floor.
The dog took a sniff of me,
Then on my leg it poured.

They gave to me a paper towel;
It soaked up most the mess.
Then what happened next to me,
Honey, you will never guess.

The Manager said I'd caused a scene,
And would I just please leave.
I never thought at my bank,
Such treatment I'd receive.

THE LORD SPEAKS:

Excuse me, Sid, may I speak up?
I couldn't help but overhear.
The attitude you've expressed just now
Is one I really fear.

What if everyone took their right
With no thought of the other one?
In our war of good over bad
No victories would be won.

Sid, you spend too much time
Asking for your right.
I'd rather see you watching for
The other needs in sight.

The Book Store

Good morning, Sir. My name is Sid,
And I've got to speak my mind.
May I sit down with you,
If some time you can find?

The bookstore you own on our block
Has caused me some concern.
I'd like to come by this afternoon.
There's much for you to learn.

This sure is a spooky place,
All the windows draped in black.
That burly guard at the door,
No brawn he seems to lack.

His office seems so full of folks;
Each one looks real tough.
I think I'll just turn around;
I've been here long enough.

Come on in? Well, I guess so.
How are you all today?
My name is Sidney, but call me Sid.
Now I'll be on my way.

Oh, yes. That's right. My concern.
I asked to share my mind.
With patience, please hear me out,
If you will be so kind?

I've a problem with your bookstore
And the books that you sell.
I'm a Christian and I'm proud of it,
As you can clearly tell.

Now, I don't doubt that you're fine folks,
And I don't want you to think
I find your books disgusting
Or that your products make me blink.

In fact, I rather like this place,
But I'd like to see you add
A religious book or two;
Then you wouldn't seem so bad.

You know, I really am a friend;
That's really why I'm here.
I've always said what I think.
In my heart, I have no fear.

THE LORD SPEAKS:

*Well, Sid, you really told them,
And tomorrow, because of you,
They will add to their book list
A Christian book or two.*

*But fearless Sid, my good man,
You've done no one any good,
For once again you caved in
When for the truth you should have stood.*

The Stop Sign

Hello, Officer. What is wrong?
You're wearing quite a frown.
Someone needs to speak to me
At the station house down town.?

Of course, I'll come, but what is wrong?
The law I never shirk.
Oh, yes, I pulled from the sign
With a squeal and a jerk.

Here I am in a strange town
And in a distant state.
I've heard about these southern boys
And an innocent stranger's fate.

I'll suppose I'll just disappear
In the smoke of a forty-four,
Leaving behind a wife and kids,
All destitute and poor.

I can see now what will happen;
It's the chain gang life for me.
By day, tied to a killer;
At night, tied to a tree.

We'll get soup for every meal,
Flavored with a shoe;
Then bug-infested cornbread
That tastes a lot like glue.

Or, I'll be dumped into a cell
And chained up to the wall,
With a homicidal maniac
Who stands up eight feet tall.

While rats and mice come crawling
All across the floor.,
Long cobwebs saggingly drape
Across the wide locked door.

Honey, I will miss you,
Never more to see your face,
For I'll suddenly disappear,
Lost without a trace.

Sonny and Sis, I love you.
Can you hear this far away?
I'm soon to be gone forever,
On this, my final day.

THE LORD SPEAKS:

Well, that was close, Sid, Old Boy!
I can't remember when,
For running through a stop sign,
The fine was only ten.

Remember what you imagined
When you felt foreboding dread?
There are folks out there living through
All the things you said.

The Flat Tire

Honey, you can't beat this day
For a pleasant cruise.
This relaxing country spin,
I knew we all could use.

We'll drive out to the game preserve
And see if we can find
Some animals we rarely see,
If you all don't mind.

Sonny, you keep a real good watch.
Sis, you can write them down.
Honey, you and I'll look, too,
As soon as we leave town.

There it is...up ahead!
There's no one else around.
Now kids, first thing you must know,
We cannot make a sound.

Now, why's that car sitting there?
We'd best slow down to see
If someone is there needing help.
I'm sure glad that it's not me.

It's lonely here, so far from town,
And you never can be sure
That they're not stopped out here
To catch us in a lure.

Hey! It's our neighbor Jimmy John!
His tire has gone flat.
Let's stop and offer him our help;
We surely can do that.

You say you need a four-way iron?
Mine I must have lost,.
And driving back into town
Would really be a cost.

Boy, John, I wish I could help,
But if I drive to town,
I'd not have time to keep our plans
And I'd let my family down.

Now if there's something else,
John, just say the word.
I'm known as one who really cares;
I know that's what you've heard.

Well, Dear, another good deed,
Although it wasn't much.
Most often though, our best help
Is just a gentle touch.

I think when we get home
We'll take some time to pray
For John and others just like him
Who do not walk Christ's way.

THE LORD SPEAKS:

Well, Sid, your neighbor made it,
Back into the town.
And, he has decided,
To your Church he won't come down.

He has decided to visit elsewhere,
Which is your church's loss.
Your self-righteous pronouncement,
Got the point across.

The Planning Board

I'm here before the Planning Board
As a spokesman for our church.
We need to get a variance
For the land on which we perch.

I know you've all heard about
The change we'd like to make,
So to better fill you in,
Your time I'd like to take.

As you well know, right next door
Is a giant softball park,
And the games on Sunday
Last a long time after dark.

Now I'm a Christian gentleman
And to fight is not my game,
So listen to my argument;
You'll find it far from lame.

First of all, it is our right
To do as we would like.
We've always done it in our way,
Ever since I was a tike.

And now you come along
To push us all around,
But you cannot control us,
No matter how the law may sound.

I have a real fine lawyer;
Slipshod Shyster is his name.
He'll fight you on the land and sea;
To him it's all the same.

He'll tie you up in court,
Then squeeze you till you're dry,
And when your town has lost this case,
For much you'll have to cry.

I am a reasonable man,
And I try to walk God's way,
But if there's something on my mind,
The truth I have to say.

I've heard it said behind your back
That each of you is a crook;
If we don't get all we want,
We'll throw at you the book.

THE LORD SPEAKS:

Sid, I'm not pleased with your work
And all that you have said.
Your permit for a hot-dog stand
Is just as good as dead.

Your threats and the blackmail
Won't point those folks to Me.
I only hope they'll understand,
In Thee, they'll not see Me.

The Mall

I'm pleased as punch to be here,
To speak to your group.
I really liked the lamb chops,
And especially, the soup.

Our downtown Chamber of Commerce
Is right to have concern
About the giant suburban mall,
So some lessons we must learn.

Three principles have guided me
On my road to great success.
Two ended up with more,
And one, it brought me less.

I'd like to share them now with you.
So, to better listen in,
Let's stop dipping in our ice cream,
Then more business we can win.

The first principle of business
Is to import all you need;
Just make sure the instructions
Are in English so folks can read.

The second principle I live by
Is to always have enough
Of all those cheaper items,
And you'll sell a lot of stuff.

The third principle to follow
Is to have a cut-rate price,
And as you speak of quality,
Present yourself as nice.

With plenty of cheap imports,
You'll always make a sale.
As you move from rags to riches,
You surely will not fail.

Yes, gentlemen of the Chamber,
And, of course, the women, too,
I have shared with you my heart,
And now I'm nearly through.

Still, I close with a warning!
Our threat remains the mall,
And if we don't do something,
Our profits soon will fall.

THE LORD SPEAKS:

Sid, the mall called a bit ago
And said they have some space,
But you'd best not tell the Chamber
You want to move your place.

I say, "Get back to the basics,
Based on God's love divine.
They emphasize doing right,
And downtown you'll do fine.

The Traffic Stop

Why, good afternoon, Officer.
I stopped when I saw your light.
I saw that fellow run the sign
As I was turning right.

What's this? You say you stopped me?
I'm Sidney; you wouldn't dare.
Why I always stop and buy a treat
From your booth out at the fair.

I admit that I was speeding,
But my reason is real good.
You see that giant engine
Underneath my ornate hood.

Now you may think a hundred,
Back on the old highway,
May be pushing the pedal just a bit,
But to this car it's only play.

Now, I know I need a license
For my old one has expired,
But Officer, I work real hard
And I always get home tired.

If you only knew all I do,
My service, is beyond compare.
Why if you were to stop by my store,
There's a free suit the size you wear.

I remember the parking tickets.
I got them right outside my store.
You'd think that an owner
Could park right by his door.

I suppose it's true they've piled up,
And three hundred seems a lot,
But I've only ever got them
Right there at that same spot.

So, Officer, I now throw myself
At the mercy of your will.
Say, can you hold this stack of cash?
I'm afraid that it may spill.

You know, it isn't often
I meet a lawman of your worth.
By the way, my store gives discounts
When my friends celebrate their birth.

THE LORD SPEAKS:

Sid, once again you've done it,
And this time you've cooked your goose.
For the reason that he stopped you,
Is your rear license plate is loose.

Now your car will be impounded,
And you soon will face the judge.
And when it comes to tickets,
His Honor will not budge.

The Election

I'm running for the school board,
And I'm prepared to stand
For what we know is right,
And what is needed in our land.

Three areas I'm therefore pushing;
Administration is a mess.
The textbooks, most inadequate
And in testing, most folks guess.

The problem is, as I see it,
Are the buildings they are in.
They say it's hard to do the work
When walls are very thin.

I support a brand new building,
And expense we will not spare.
It will be the pride of this our state,
A school beyond compare.

The textbooks are clearly shabby,
Some of them, three years old.
Most pictures are in black and white;
At least, that's what I'm told.

There is a brand new publisher
My brother-in-law works for;
I suggest we buy all brand new
And toss the old ones out the door.

Our testing scores are going down,
And I've an answer for this need.
Let's open up the purse strings,
And our money kids will heed.

One dollar for each grade of *A*,
Fifty cents for a *B*;
A *C* will earn a quarter,
And then good grades we'll see.

So, vote for me, good old Sid.
I can do the job, I can.
Yes, vote for me, good old Sid.
I'm your one and only man.

Cut, OK gang, that will wrap.
The commercial will be great
My opponent, she can't top this.
For my victory, I can't wait.

THE LORD SPEAKS:

Too bad about you losing, Sid.
One vote, at least, you got.
Do you know what the problem was?
Your commercial was not too hot.

As parents heard you speak your piece,
Love for kids, it was not heard,
So when it came the time to vote,
Your support, it never stirred.

The Canoe

Yes Sir, I built it myself,
It didn't take too long.
Now if you are interested,
You can buy it for a song.

Some folks wouldn't even try
To build this kind of canoe.
They'd be afraid it would not float.
But I see that person is not you.

The plans? You'd like to see my plans?
Well, Sir, let me make your day.
Before you sets a handmade boat;
Designed along the way.

Plans just confuse most folks;
It's best to start right in.
Oh! I forgot to tell you, Sir,
That Daniel Boone was one of my kin.

Well, if you think I need to,
I'll tell you what I did.
But, just so folks won't copy me,
You keep it under lid.

I used the finest wood,
No matter what the price;
However, some that I bought
Had been purchased twice.

I made sure any nail holes
Were tightly filled with glue;
I used the kind cobblers use
When working on a shoe.

Sure it's strong. My rubber soles
Have never come apart.
The fifteen plugs will not work loose;
There is no way they can start.

So, Fellow, what do you think?
Do you want this canoe?
I won't let it go too cheap,
So keep that point in view.

No, wait! There's got to be a way
To make this a special deal,
So open up your money belt
And give those bills a peel.

Now, don't be afraid to call
If I can help you out;
Remember to never drop the boat,
The wood may not be stout.

That's because there are some cracks,
But if you soak it overnight,
The all the cracks will swell shut,
And the canoe will be all right.

Hello? Oh Hello, how is the canoe?
You say, you launched it yesterday,
And after paddling for ten minutes,
The bottom fell away?

Well, I do not know what went wrong.
Did you soak it long enough?
You know that gym shoe glue
Can be awfully tricky stuff.

THE LORD SPEAKS:

OK, Sid, I'm cutting in
On your little plan.
Did you truly, truly think
That you could fool the man?

You built your boat for the land
There was no way that it would float.
And over in the Small Claims Court,
You'll lose both your shirt and coat.

The Sale

Sid, I'm counting on your best
When tomorrow you see the man.
If anyone here can make the sale,
Sid, I know you can.

So get a real good night's sleep,
Then show him all our line.
There's no doubt you're our man;
We know you'll do just fine.

It's ten o'clock, I'll go to bed
And get the rest I need.
I'll roll out early from my nest,
And my notes again I'll read.

I wish I had a bit more time
To polish up my speech,
But tomorrow's coming quick enough.
Honey, the light cord, can you reach?

Ninety-nine thousand six hundred and nine.
There's sheep exiting my eyeball.
I'm wide awake at quarter past three;
It's my fourth trip down the hall.

Honey's snoring in the bed,
Sleeping since ten thirty-eight.
I can't believe I'm doing this
It must have been something I ate.

I've searched the fridge again and again;
There's nothing I want to eat.
If I don't get to sleep real soon,
The coming dawn I'll greet.

There's no way I'll make the sale
Without some hours of sleep,
But there's no way out of this,
The appointment I've got to keep.

Oh, Lord, tell me what's wrong;
This has never happened before.
I just looked at the clock right now,
And, Lord, it's nearly four.

I can't get the sale off my mind
I keep running through my pitch.
If I can just make the sale,
My commission will be rich.

THE LORD SPEAKS:

Good morning, Mr. Early Bird.
I see you were up all night.
For someone with a great big sale,
You sure do look a fright.

Remember what you read last night
From Matthew 6 and thirty-four.
Instead of sleeping long and sound,
You were pacing on the floor.

Do you know what you just lost
By hours of worry and fret?
I looked ahead to when you meet,
And, an order you won't get.

You'll fall asleep in his chair
While he is on the phone.
When you awake much later on,
He's left you all alone.

Now Sid, you won't lose your job,
So don't lose another night;
Just the next time you go to bed,
Try to do it right.

Just leave tomorrow where it is;
Today's enough for you,
And know that when tomorrow comes,
I'll be right there to help you through.

The Work Day

All right, folks, let's settle down;
We've got a lot to do.
This is an annual work-day,
And we're here 'til we get through.

With our dear pastor out of town,
I'll have to be in charge,
For when it comes to energy,
My reservoir is large.

I've thought this through carefully
And if we do this right,
We'll be finished long before
The sun is lost from sight.

I've divided up the workload
So all will have a share.
I know you're ready to leap to the fray;
There's plenty for you there.

I've asked our Pinford Cruet
To downstairs take a group.
They won't complain I am sure;
They'll be right near the soup.

Oh, that's right, we've planned a lunch.
We'll break for it at noon.,
So, Friends, you'd best come hastily
When you hear me bang a spoon.

Figbert Fitzhugh will take the roof,
Berford Barnes will sweep the floor,
Carleen Croup will take the nursery,
And Torrence Tripp will paint the door.

The pews belong to A.C. Dipples.
The pulpit to Blixfield Plox;
The piano goes to Alton Cree,
And I'll reset the clocks.

Well, now, let's all get to work,
Everyone to his task.
If you will work to your capacity,
That's all that I can ask.

Say, I need some help with my job;
I've chipped my right thumbnail.
The pain has slowed my progress;
And I'm working like a snail.

THE LORD SPEAKS:

Well, once again, Sid, old boy,
You've wormed out of some work,
And once again folks are forced
To do that which you shirk.

I'd like to see you volunteer
To do something on your own,
For it's getting oh so tiresome,
Hearing your mournful moan.

The Membership Board

As Chairman of the Membership Board,
This meeting I will start.
And, Pastor, please don't take offense
Of what we say to heart.

We know you are a real fine man
And your ministry here is great,
But an issue large we now do have,
Which I, for us, will state.

The crowd is growing every week;
Good folks are coming in.
But the kind of folks that we need most,
Their numbers, they are thin.

The standard for our membership
To us is very clear,
And most of those who now have joined
Have missed it, we all fear.

We're looking for folks to come
Whose lifestyle will compare
With those who live around the church
And name-brand clothes do wear.

We need those "old family" names
On our membership list,
So when they all have passed away,
Their money will be missed.

Why, just last week, right up in front,
You took Parkwell Piffle in,
And when it comes to contests,
No prizes will he win.

Piffle has an infamous name
That will never make us proud;
Besides, his orange leisure suit
Seems awfully, awfully loud.

Yes, Pastor, careful we must be,
Or we will quickly find
The rich folk moving on from us,
Leaving our treasury in a bind.

We're called to reach out to the lost,
But they need not be the poor;
We're better off if we just see
New rich folks at the door.

THE LORD SPEAKS:

Sid, I like your church the way it is;
Don't try to spoil it now,
For if you try to drive folks out,
You'll stir up quite a row.

Unknown to all you uppity-ups,
There's a unity here I find,
For while you're off complaining
They sing, Blest Be the Ties That Bind.

The Fellowship Committee

Chairman of the Fellowship Committee.
Sid, that title is a plum.
And as the pastor said, when he called,
"Sid, your turn has come."

He suggested that I organize
A family one on one.
For some reason way beyond me,
He thinks that would be fun.

I'll select first some folks for us;
That's really only fair.
We have so much love to give
And with others we must share.

Gastrick Piffle is a nerd,
So he will never do.
Ritzwell Fillmore burps when he eats,
And his other manners, they are few.

Garland Dripple took my place
As soloist in the choir,
And Sonny, as his lawn mower,
He refused to hire.

Clasket Tupper took his time
When last I said, "Hello".
He's not the one that I'd eat with,
Since his greeting was too slow.

Bilford Basswell sits in my pew,
Although he knows it's mine,
And Bilford's wife Boxella
Greases her face to a shine.

Oxford Dipp thinks he's cool;
His family bought the door
When the church's kitchen needed it.
He makes me feel so poor.

Pastor, this is Fellowship Chairman Sid.
I've got a sad report.
The "one on one" family mix,
With regret we must abort.

I've reviewed the church family list,
And it's sad to say, but true.
The people here can't get along,
Except for me and you.

THE LORD SPEAKS:

Excuse Me, Sid, It's Me, the Lord.
May I cut in on your call?
If I were you, I'd overlook
Those problems that are small.

No one's perfect in your world,
So as brothers you must meet.
Oh, by the way, Chairman Sid,
Put on your shoes. I smell your feet!

The Neighbor

Cumquat Squirsh, what a name,
And he's a neighbor of mine to boot.
There's are times if I had a gun,
Those dogs of his I'd shoot.

His cats are always in my yard
Digging in my flower bed.
I can't ever look at them
Without turning red.

Now, don't look at me and shake your head;
There's times you feel this way.
The difference is I'm not afraid
To say just what I say.

Of course, I'd not want Cumquat
To know just how I feel,
For I always try to get along,
Although he's such a heel.

There was a time years ago
When I called Squirsh a friend,
But that was before the dogs and cats
And the fence he would not mend.

Since that time we rarely speak;
At least you won't hear me.
If I had a way and a chance,
His face I'd never see.

In spite of all he's done to me,
I pray for him once a week.
I pray his sour hardened heart
On the Lord soon would seek.

If he'd get right with the Lord,
His dogs and cats would go,
And then I'd be more inclined
The love of God to show.

Of course, his faults are many more.
He mows his lawn once a week
In the early morning hours
When the sun just starts to peek.

I could tell you much, much more,
But I have made my case,
So if I were you, I'd stay away
And not go near his place.

THE LORD SPEAKS:

Sid, old boy, I've got you now.
You don't live by my law.
As I often told the Pharisees,
I won't tolerate that flaw.

Everything I ever did
Was for both friend and foe;
So, Sid, if we're to get along,
Love to Cumquat, you must show.

The Evaluation

Evaluate Nimbus Quimple?
Well, Pastor, I'll do my best,
Although I am the finest choice
When looking at the rest.

As the former teacher of the Bible class,
Where Nimbus now is boss,
You can be sure I'll clearly see
If his work is gain or loss.

First, as for his educational skill,
There's no need for alarm;
He attended a one-room school each day,
Just a mile from his farm.

Although his speech is adequate,
There's times when he can't speak.
I'm not sure if he thinks too slow,
Or if his vocal chords are weak.

He rarely reads the Bible
When we meet to study and pray.
That's not to say I doubt his faith
Or his walking of Christ's way.

He seems to always question
What the Word is all about,
And speaking for some others,
His questions cause some doubt.

Well, there it is, dear Pastor;
I've laid it on the line.
Although there is some concern,
I suppose he's doing fine.

Though I'm willing to step in,
Let there be no doubt.
Nimbus, I'm sure, will do all right,
If he'd let me help him out.

THE LORD SPEAKS:

Sid, whose class are you in?
Your description doesn't fit.
Nimbus to the state college went,
And with teachers made a hit.

When he's quiet during study time,
He's letting others speak,
And he asks for different readers
In his class every week.

The questions cause the class to think
Of how they really feel.
There's no doubt in My mind
His faith in Me is real.

The problem here is yours, not his.
You look through jealous eye,
So take another look at him;
He's really quite a guy.

The revival

Guess what, Honey! I've been asked
To serve on a planning board
To bring revival to our town
And win folks to the Lord.

I told them I surely would,
But now I do not know.
Is that the way to reach the lost
And help our church to grow?

While driving home I thought it out.
What would the neighbors say
If I became a revivalist
And on emotions play?

All the people on our street
Know to church I go,
But, Honey, let's not go overboard
When we our faith should show.

Take your sister Ferina Sue.
She's got to raise her hand
Every time the choir sings
"On Christ the Solid Rock I Stand".

Then she shouts, "Praise the Lord,"
When someone testifies,
And when there's hurting in the church,
She kneels right down and cries.

Or, look at Jim, my bowling friend
Since he was saved last year.
All he talks about is Christ;
That's all I ever hear..

Yes, I know he's won a few,
But that's only because he tries
To convert everyone he meets,
When he drives or flies.

I can't believe my sister Lil
Across the sea would go.
Remember when she told us that
God's will she now did know.

A doctor with a future bright!
Can you believe her role
Treating snake and lion bites
In a forgotten jungle hole?

Then there's your nephew Billy Bob,
Baking in the desert sun
Teaching Navahos how to read.
Now that can't be much fun!

He had it made where he was,
The youngest professor there.
I told him to look at what he had;
He said he didn't care.

Ferina, Jim, Lil, and Bob,
All carried away.
Now, Honey, if that's what it takes,
That game I'll never play.

You know, as I think of it,
Revivals did them in,
With all that talk of sacrifice
And fighting against sin.

THE LORD SPEAKS:

Well, Sid, I guess you won't be there
When revival hits this town,
And for others it's just as well;
You'd view it with a frown.

But when you're next at the Sports Dome,
Screaming off your head,
I'll take some time to remind you
Of what you just have said.

The Helper

Hello, Sid, this is Pastor.
How are you today?
I'm doing well, thank you,
You're sounding good, but say,

I've not time to chit chat,
So I'll say what's on my mind.
Now that you're the deacon-Chairman,
A helper you must find.

Honey, guess what I've been asked to do.
You'll not believe your ears.
I've got to run downtown today
To see old Cyril Meers.

You remember him, don't you?
He lives in a shopping cart.
Pastor wants me to help him out,
And I don't know where to start.

As well you know he's filthy;
His facial dirt is deep.
I don't know how to touch him,
And far away still keep.

I just can't do it, Honey
That dirty job's not mine;
I'll get someone else to do it.
What about Philthorpe Pline?

Hi, Philthorpe, this is Sid.
The church has got a need;
We've a member who lives downtown
Whose spirit needs a feed.

I've thought long and hard on this,
And you're the best man for the task.
There's not another man around
That I would like to ask.

Well, Phil, how about it,
Can the church count on you?
Of course, you must tell me what you did
When finished you are through.

I'd really love to do it myself;
But I haven't got the time;
If you only knew all the tasks I do,
My praises you would chime.

THE LORD SPEAKS:

Well, Sid, ring-a-ling
Is all you'll get from me;,
And I'd say those praising days
Are days you'll never see.

Remember the black man Simon,
When he had a chance to serve,
Although forced he did it willingly,
And Sid, that takes a lot of nerve.

The Cousin

Honey, here's a letter you should read.
It's from my cousin Crick
From Hooper Hollow, Iowa.
That boy is such a hick.

He wants us all to visit him
And spend a few days on his farm.
Well, I suppose we could find the time;
It wouldn't do any harm.

Dear Crick, this is Cousin Sid.
We'll soon be on our way.
We'll stay with you at least a week,
And be very glad to pay.

We know you're in troubled times,
With prices and drought last Fall,
So we'd better come in a month,
Before you lose it all.

Now Crick, I hope you've quit that group
That got you in your fix.
Farmers fighting for family farms,
You know land and law don't mix.

The last time I saw anything of you,
You were there on TV
Speaking out for farm families.
Crick, you embarrassed me.

Now, we'll come to visit if we won't hear
Any talk about your farm;
As far as Honey and I are concerned,
Your fear just breeds alarm.

With that all done, can we see
A baby pig be born?
I'd also like for Sonny and Sis
To run in your fields of corn.

I sure do hope your pond is full
Of fish to catch and eat,
And what about that neighbor
The one who is so neat?

He's a first class farmer.
From him you can learn,
The ins and outs of farming,
So more money you can earn.

THE LORD SPEAKS:

Sid, don't send that letter;
It's not that way anymore.
Crick's lost all but his house,
And he's feeling mighty poor.

His pond dried up and is no longer there.
The corn all went to the bank.
His neighbor that you liked so well
Died of the poison that he drank.

His wife and kids moved to the city,
With her folks some time they'll spend,
Until Crick's got it together,
And for the family, he can send.

Crick's lost it all but his pride,
And hopes you understand
That speaking out may cost a lot,
But still you take a stand.

The Ad

Honey, he's at it once again.
A full-page ad this time.
When will that loony ever learn,
On top he'll never climb?

My store is the best in this town;
He can't achieve my fame.
Well, I can play hardball, too
If that will be his game.

He's doomed to certain failure, Honey;
He never will succeed.
Just look at what he offers here;
Now listen as I read.

"A One-year Long Guarantee
On Each Appliance Sold".
If I gave out such a warranty,
I'd be out in the cold.

His suits are all first quality,
No seconds on his racks.
Doesn't he know that folks can't feel
The difference on their backs.

My seconds all look real good
And we snip each loose thread,
So I'll not upgrade my quality,
No matter what is said.

I've got to try to stop this man,
And I won't count the cost.
If I allow him to have his way,
My business will be lost.

I'll have a giant ad next week
That will blow him out to sea;
Then everyone in town will know
The best in business is me.

Dear hometown friends, this is old Sid.
An outsider has come to town.
He offers you a warranty,
But he'll only let you down.

I question, too, his quality,
And I've seen his kind before.
Fly-by-night, here-then-gone.
You'd best shop at my store.

THE LORD SPEAKS:

Sid, is it really your desire
To run an ad this way?
It seems to me that jealousy
And revenge rules your day.

Just be content to do your best
And change because you must,
For if your quality you don't up,
In sales, you'll eat his dust.

The Youth Pastor

Honey, I just talked to Marple McGlide,
And the Search Committee's through.
Guess who they want to call to our church!
Their choices must have been few.

As for our next youth pastor,
They're inviting Charmwell's son.
Who'd want to have a pastor
Who has the name of Bun?

Bun Charmwell is an OK kid.
But he'll never make the grade.
Growing up in our hometown,
Few marks he ever made.

I've drawn up reasons some
Why he will never work;
Someone has got to speak out now,
So my duty I'll not shirk.

First of all, there's high school sports;
He never was a star
On any team he played on.
That says he won't go far.

Just being a player on the team
Is surely not enough;
We need someone to push out front,
For life's pressures sure are tough.

My next concern's a big one;
It's the college where he went.
He stayed right here at his home,
Instead of away being sent.

Now, that's not to say the Bible School
Downtown is not much good,
But I'm not sure much can be learned
In small buildings made of wood.

Last, but not least, he's a local boy,
Not one who's been around.
The one who leads the youth of our church
Must have covered lots of ground.

The world's far bigger than it seems;
Experience is the trick.
We need to find a city boy,
Not just a small town hick.

THE LORD SPEAKS:

You know, Sid, it sure is strange.
By your standard I would fail,
For when it comes to hometowns,
From a tiny town I hail.

You'd better set your sights on Me
When looking for a man,
Or even a lady, possibly,
If you think you can.

The Golfers

Honey, it's Farnsworth Fiddle.
He wants to golf a round.
"Let's shoot eighteen," he said, "then lunch;
My golf clubs I have found."

Now I know from me he borrowed them
At least two years ago,
But I've not had time to golf since then,
As you yourself well know.

Who else, you say? He mentioned them,
But you like neither one.
Hilborn Fleeg and Riddle Fiddle,
Farnsworth's oldest son.

Sure, Hilborn has a filthy mouth,
But, Honey, most folks do;
So, I'll meet them at the car,
And then he won't see you.

Young Riddle Fiddle has not seen Sis
Since I threatened to break his face,
And anyway a round of golf
Would show I'm a man of grace.

They like me, I know they do,
And sure they're often jerks
But everyone alive these days
Has abnormal quirks.

Oh, Honey, after I'm gone,
Call up Blissfield Clum.
Tell him I became involved
And to his house can't come.

I know how he depends on me,
But often I need a break,
Or old and crippled Blissfield
All my time will take.

THE LORD SPEAKS:

Sid, I often ate with sinners,
But I did it for their good,
And never did they stop Me
From doing what I should.

Farnsworth's going to keep your clubs,
And the others will talk trash,
And while Blissfield trying to fix the stairs
He will fall and both legs smash.

Those fellows aren't your brothers in Christ,
But have a good time if you can,
Knowing full well, all the time
From a ministry you ran.

The Bus

I sure do hope he won't sit here!
His clothes, they sure do stink.
I hope no one sees me get off,
I know what they would think.

I can't believe she needs the car
I thought she liked being home.
So, here I sit on a bus
As through the streets we roam.

I can't believe the way they look;
You'd think they'd have some pride.
If I had to dress like that,
I'd just squat down and hide.

Oh no! Not here! Not on my seat!
A diaper you can't change!
At home, when it came to that,
I kept well out of range.

Purple hair! Half shaved off!
Your finger nails are green.
You want to sit with me
Young lady, I might be seen!

So move on down to the back,
And take another seat.
I hope and pray someone like you,
My Sonny will never meet.

Lady, will you move your kid
Up to another seat!
He's always looking at my suit,
And besides I smell his feet.

You'd think he never took a bath
He's dirt from head to toe.
I'm sorry, but I have no choice;
Your boy, he's got to go.

This bus is full but still they come.
There ought to be a law
That limits those who ride a bus
To those without a flaw.

Although I've never ridden before,
I surely have the right
To board a bus again sometime
With these folks far from sight.

Driver, why do you pick them up?
I'd think you'd have some pride.
Don't you have some say
In the type of folks that ride?

If I were you I'd pass them by;
Surely they could walk.
Why, most of these are real low-lifes
You can tell by how they talk.

Here's my corner. Say, Driver, stop!
You boob! You went right by!
Forget the cord that rings the bell,
For I know you heard my cry.

Now three blocks I have to walk;
This really makes my day.
On top of all that I've gone through,
For this ride I have to pay.

THE LORD SPEAKS:

So, Sid, you've ridden on a bus.
That really was a treat.
You rarely get such an excellent chance
Other kinds of folks to meet.

These are folks who dream like you
Of having a better chance.
Could it be I put you there
So I could your life enhance?

The Christmas List

I've got to trim my Christmas list
A little more this year,
Or I will go so deep in debt;
Alas, how do I fear.

There must be someone I can drop
Who will not miss my gift.
There needs to be but two or three
Whose names I can safely lift.

I can think of one who comes to mind,
My worthless brother-in-law Ferd.
He may not come to town this year;
At least, that's what I heard.

I've been wanting to drive his Corvette
That he stores in our backyard;
I can't take him off my list
Or my asking will be hard.

Old Hopeford I could always drop.
Let's see, his last name's Snell.
It seems he's getting awfully weak,
For his health is not too well.

Our men's group has been counting on
Being guests at his supper club,
And if he doesn't get a gift
He'll think that him I snub.

I know, I'll drop Ferina Sue;
She preaches about the Lord.
My sister-in-law is a real nut,
And her sermons leave me bored.

She always speaks of sacrifice,
So she'll get her chance this year
To sacrificially miss a gift
She's so meek I have no fear.

Hello, Ferina, this is Sid.
How's it going over there?
Oh, the Lord just quietly spoke to me,
And His message I will share.

He said He's not at all pleased
With the Christmas gifts we share,
So I've sent back the gift for you;
I knew you would not care.

THE LORD SPEAKS:

Sid, you're right, she does not care,
But this news will warm your soul;
She bought you what you really want,
A Felix Fillmore Fly Rod Pole.

She thought about your vision of late
And believes that it is true;
She's calling now all your friends
So your gifts this year will be few.

The Graveyard

Now when we get to the graveyard
And I park the car,
I don't want you wandering.
Don't go very far.

We've come here for a very good purpose,
So by my side please stay.
We've come to revisit the graves of our kin
On this Memorial Day.

Now the relatives all lying here
Were each one tried and true,
And I am proud that my memories
I can pass right on to you.

Right there lies great Uncle Spork.
He was a real tall man,
Until he played Blind Man's Bluff
With a ceiling fan.

Wait! There's no need to think the worst.
He just took a nasty rap,
But from that day he was called
A slow, dim-witted sap.

He'd wander up and down the street
Asking for the time,
Which he would take in exchange
For a single dime.

Over there Cousin Quillard lies;
He was a good old boy.
As a matter of fact, Family,
He was done in by a toy.

While slyly stealing down the stair
Very late one night to eat,
He did not see a roller skate,
But his Maker he did meet.

Well, that was quite a inspiring tour.
Aren't you glad you came?
I think we had so much fun;
Next year we'll do the same.

It's always good to remember
Those who have gone on before.
Now, to the Lincoln let's all return,
And hurry back to the store.

THE LORD SPEAKS:

Too bad you wasted your lunchtime,
Though the visit it was right.
You missed the point of memory,
Notwithstanding it was well in sight.

Those who have gone on before
Should be known for what they tried
To pass on to those whom they loved,
And not just how they died.

The Invitation

Say, for the invitation I give thanks,
But I simply cannot join.
I've sent my application in
At the Pork Tenderloin.

It's the newest modern Supper Club
In this part of the state,
And excited I am justly so,
That I can hardly wait.

Your service club is fine for most,
But it's surely not right for me,
For I'm a man of substance
And your membership is free.

The thousand dollar entry fee
To the Pork Tenderloin Club
Will guarantee elbows rich
Every night a chance to rub.

You see, I'm a real important person
In the program of my church,
And if I don't get to know the rich,
I'll leave fund-raising in the lurch.

As you can tell by my looks,
I belong at the top,
So it wouldn't be fair to our church
If my lifestyle were to stop.

There is a man you could call;
He may just join your group.
You'll find his name is Potwell Cling
And he owns the Chicken Soup.

His diner is on he smallish side
And serves food to the poor;
I've never been inside the place,
But I hear it's a real fine store.

Potwell's into this service thing;
He gives it all the time,
But for me, you see, it's not the way
Up the social ladder climb.

Actually, I've made the better choice
And it took a lot of nerve.
Instead of serving other folks,
I'd rather let them serve.

THE LORD SPEAKS:

Ah, the Pork Tenderloin.
That's quite a place to go.
The food is great, I am sure,
But the service is real slow.

You see, many refuse to work there;
The snootiness they hate.
So when you order a prime rib,
Be prepared, Sidney, to wait.

The Guests

Tomorrow night is New Year's Eve.
Honey, where would you like to go?
Whom could we invite to go along
To dinner, bowling, and a show?

This will be a special time;
It comes but once a year.
Our guests must be a careful choice,
So a bad time we'll not fear.

Winthrop Wallenbeel and his wife?
Well, Honey, I don't know;
I've heard he's very good at the lanes.
Why, he could be a pro.

If I had the time and the money he has,
I could be a bowling great;
So until I can bowl as good as he,
Their invitation must wait.

Manny and Margarita Moskowitz
Came to my mind, too,
But in public we cannot be seen
With a Chicano and a Jew.

Now there is not a hateful bone
In my body, oh so neat,
But going out with those two
We don't know whom we'll meet.

I've ruled out Fillbert and Fanny.
Fillbert almost took my place,
And when it comes to singing,
No one takes my space.

I'm always in place in the choir loft
So all can see I'm there;
It wouldn't do to let folks think
About my job I do not care.

I think we'll go by ourselves.
No one seems good enough
To spend an evening with us two;
Our standards, they are tough.

But that's all right, Honey, dear.
God demands an equal yoke,
So to keep our faith being pure,
We'll avoid inferior folk.

THE LORD SPEAKS:

Happy New Year, Sidney!
It won't be that for me,
For you won't change your stubborn ways
And your problems I can see.

Pride, prejudice, and power, all three,
Guide you that's for sure,
And until you can see that,
Your holiness is impure.

The Diagnosis

Well, Doc and the Missus, we sure are glad
You both could come tonight.
Honey and I were just now saying
The way you're treated isn't right.

I've watched how folks have used you
To get things done for free;
But you can fully count on this,
You'll not get that treatment from me.

Please pass the mashed potatoes,
And the gravy, too.
That reminds me of a problem
I've got and it's not new.

Do potatoes have cholesterol?
My level may be high.
Any ideas on what needs to be done?
Is there a diet I can try?

Could you pour me a little milk.
My wrist is very sore.
I've babied it for some time now,
But still I'm feeling poor.

While you're here, why not take a look.
Is there something you can see?
Should I just live with it,
Like I do with my knee?

My knee, oh, it's really bad!
In fact, it's hurting now.
It all goes back to the farm
And a certain milking cow.

Do you suppose wrapping it
Will help to ease the pain,
Or would an operation
Help me relief to gain?

Well, thanks for coming over.
Come back again real soon.
Oh, by the way, the office call
I made for Monday noon,

I think that I will cancel it;
My problems, they are small.
You're much too busy anyway;
When I need you I will call.

THE LORD SPEAKS:

Sid, guess who saw through you
As you sat at your meal.
The doc surely understood
The way you really feel.

Oh, by the way, old Sid,
You're in for quite a thrill,
For while you were talking there,
Doc decided to send you a bill.

The Candidate

Well, men, we've been asked again to pick
Our candidate for this year
To be our city's leader great,
And again we'll fail, I fear.

Some say to pick a founding father;
Their stories have been told.
Even so, I must recite them,
If I may be so bold.

The oldest, Isaiah Tribble,
Was the tallest of the bunch,
And what made him all so different
Was what he had for lunch.

He would not eat any kind of meat,
Just veggies, fruit, and cheese.
Is it any wonder at one hundred and ten
He had arthritis in both knees.

Then, we have Jeremiah Tribble,
The second oldest son.
His nose was always in a book,
So he never was much fun.

He studied hard for many years
While his brothers did the work.
Although a real good doctor;
Other duties he did shirk.

Ezekiel Tribble, the muscle man,
By that nickname he was known,
Owned the biggest biceps
Our town has ever grown.

Flexing muscles was his game
While out working in the hay;
Although, he shared all he cut
Each and every day.

As we have seen, each of them
Had a weird quirk,
And because of what they were,
Their names we have to shirk.

So, I humbly offer you my name.
As you know, I eat real meat,
And I'm far too busy to read
Or exercise in the heat.

THE LORD SPEAKS:

*Sid, any of those brothers
Deserves to take the prize.
Besides, you'll not be a leader true,
However loud your cries.*

*The Tribble brothers were all right
And left far more than lore.
In fact, a great-great grandson likes your Sis,
And he'll soon be knocking at your door.*

The Yard

What's this? An invitation
To our neighbor's house?
To enjoy his newly landscaped yard?
Boy, he's such a louse.

He's only got that beautiful yard
Because I lost the case,
And now he wants to rub it in
And put me in my place.

Because the lot had been overgrown,
The judge let me off the hook.
He said if that he weren't so nice,
At me he'd throw the book.

He said to remove what I'd dumped there,
And that's all I'd have to do.
Little did he realize
All that he put me through.

Sonny's little three-wheeler track
Was harder than it looked.
When I saw the rocks and logs,
I knew my goose was cooked.

I had forgotten all that we'd hauled in
In just the past year.
When we started working on the track,
It took a week to clear.

By a load in a wheelbarrow, one at a time,
I took that pile down.
All I have left to remind me of it,
Are white gym shoes, now turned brown.

Oh, yes, I know several times
He's asked to make things right,
But I can't ever forgive him,
So I'll stay out of sight.

Anyway, Honey, if I go
He'll just look at me and gloat
So I'll stay right here at home
And keep digging on my moat.

THE LORD SPEAKS:

Sid, I said in Matthew Six,
Verses fourteen and fifteen,
That forgiveness must come from you
Or from Me it won't be seen.

Even then I'm stretching this
To include you, that's true,
For you can be sure beyond a doubt,
The sin's not with him, but you.

You'd better go to his house now
And ask that he forgive.
You have the sin of selfish pride
And with that I cannot live.

You know I can't tolerate sin,
So I've told you what to do;
Now do it, Sid, before it's too late
And I have to settle accounts with you.

The Homeless

You know, Pastor, that's interesting,
But I can't see a way
That I can easily help you out,
No matter what you say.

Sure, it's sad about the folks
Who sleep outside at night,
But I don't see what I can do
To make the problem right.

First of all, they like it there;
If not, they'd find a room.
I've heard it said for them a house
Seems too much like a tomb.

Why, yesterday, while waiting long
For a cab to pick me up,
A street person came right up to me,
Holding out a cup.

I did not need a drink right then,
But I thanked him just the same.
Of course, he couldn't fool me
I saw right through his game.

That drink which he had offered me
Would have cost at least a buck.
Besides, I'd have caught some disease;
It would be just my luck.

Pastor, just as I had left the cab,
I bumped into a cart
Pushed slowly by a little old lady.
Her looks gave me a start.

Now rummage sales aren't my thing
So I quickly turned away;
I told her that I'd send my wife
Later on that day.

A level-headed approach to this
Would be to buy a boat.
Then load them up and sail them south
Where none would need a coat.

The beach could be their bedroom,
The sand a fine bedstead,
So when the tide comes rushing in
They'd have a water bed.

THE LORD SPEAKS:

Sid, you know what bothers Me
About your attitude?
When it comes to helping needy folks,
You're awfully, awfully rude.

Remember that cup of water cool
I spoke of in the Word.
You've never let its meaning true
In your heart of hearts be stirred.

The Poultry Nest

Oh how I love this little town.
The shops are all so neat,
And coming here once a year
For us is quite a treat.

I think the place I like the most
Is Pillards Poultry Nest,
The free refills on all the food
Is what I like the best.

I start with their luscious salad bar
And pile the lettuce up,
Drenching all with a rich French sauce
That I measure by the cup.

On the plate and around the edge
I scoop the salad treats;
Side by side they jiggle off
As we return to our seats.

It isn't long and in they come
With Pillard's Pullet Pie;
It's filled with pieces of the bird,
A true feast to the eye.

Now when I dive into this dish,
I pack it way down deep,
For coming out is still more food,
So I some room must keep.

Then out comes on a giant plate
The specialty of the place.
For Pillard's Pickled Poultry Pieces,
On the table we make the space.

They're soaked in a special sauce
Then fried so deep in lard;
When this delicacy arrives at the table,
Each piece is brown and hard.

First, I soak up all the juice
Dropping from the plate,
Using Pillard's plain pastry;
Now I can hardly wait.

I pick a leg and then a thigh
And work my way around,
Until I've eaten all there is
And no more can be found.

After eating two whole birds,
I top this little meal,
By visiting the dessert bar,
That's shaped just like a wheel.

Then I waddle out to our car,
And say this little prayer,
Thank you, Lord, for helping me,
Not overeat in there.

THE LORD SPEAKS:

Well, Sid a long, long time ago,
When I was here on earth;
There were lots and lots of folks,
Who had an enlarged girth.

They sat at many banquets,
That offered all that folks could eat.
And I watched them keep a-gobbling,
After most folks left their seat.

My friend, you have a problem,
With which you must deal.
Now don't look at me like that,
Grab your tummy Sid, and feel!

The Garden

Hey, look, the "Beginning Bean Book".
Honey, this is a find!
For getting help in gardening,
This book is one-of-a-kind.

I know this year, I'll have success,
I'll have the best in town,
A garden to please the green thumb
With doubtless great renown.

Let's see, it's February now,
And the ground is frozen still.
Another month and it will thaw;
At least, I think it will.

I have lots of preparation time
To get into the soil,
But soon I'll give the tractor green
A tune up and change of oil.

Well, look at that, will you, Sis.
It's nearly April First,
And for some homemade carrot juice
I'm getting quite a thirst.

I'd better get the tractor out
And choose my garden spot.
The Bean Book says to always pick
Out the best, most perfect spot.

Honey, it sure got early warm.
Who'd think it was May 15?
It's going to be a hot one,
The worst I've ever seen.

I think I'd best cut the size
Of the garden that we plant;
We're going to have to water much,
For the rain it will be scant.

The rain sure seems to never end;
It's now June twenty-five.
I'm afraid that all I'd like to plant
In this wet ground won't thrive.

Well, just in case, I'll hold it off
'Til I see the weather break;
Then I'll put it in for sure,
But for now a nap I'll take.

THE LORD SPEAKS:

*Well, Sid, too bad about your carrot juice.
No homemade brew you'll taste,
And Sid, as a matter of fact,
There's no need for haste.*

*You missed your chance to plant this year
Your green thumb has turned brown.
Don't dig now for it's far too late;
You might as well lie down.*

The Leak

Honey, call the plumber back.
I can fix that leak myself.
Remember when I bought that book
And laid it on the shelf.

The salesman said to do what it said,
And you can fix any leak.
Besides, those plumbers take too long;
We can't wait for a week.

Now, Sonny, you hold the book
And the flashlight, too.
It won't be long, the book tells me,
And we will be all through.

Now when I squeeze behind those pipes,
You hand me my biggest wrench.
It's lying up behind the saw
Over on the old work bench.

Let me see, if I ease my head
Between wall and sewer drain,
I can reach this troublesome toilet leak
And much time I will gain.

Now, Sonny, hand me up the wrench
And light page thirty-three.
Over a bit to the right;
There, now I can see.

If I hang my leg on that pipe
And reach around that line,
The wrench will reach to the leak
And soon all will be fine.

With just a twist to the left
Oops, no to the right it should be.
Water's spraying faster now;
It's pouring down on me.

Sonny, I have dropped the wrench!
Can you see where it fell?
While you're down there on the floor,
Upstairs will you please yell!

Tell Sis and Honey to stay away
From the toilet in the hall!
One flush and your dear old dad
Will surely catch it all.

Sonny, aim the light back here;
It seems that I am stuck
Hand the light back to me,
Then go call a fire truck.

Tell them your dad's head is caught
Between a sewer pipe and wall,
And just a little tug from them
Will pull me out, that's all.

Honey, draw another bath;
The odor's still too strong.
My skin is wrinkled like a prune;
I can't stay in for long.

The plumber has done the pipe repair,
And the mason fixed the wall.
That little job I said I could do
Turned out to be not small.

THE LORD SPEAKS:

Well, Sid, there is a lesson here
And the hard way you have learned.
There are limits to what a man can do'
And special talents must be earned.

You can't act like you know it all.
I'd rather see you be
One who needs another man,
Whose Creed's not I, but we.

The Suitcase

Honey, I'm sure I have everything
That's needed for this trip.
If there is anything else I need,
I'll call then you can ship.

Help me now to load my bag,
The one that's extra large.
That one-of-a-kind carrying case
Is shaped just like a barge.

It's locks are made of Toledo steel;
One key unlocks them all.
The heavy duty frame won't crack
Even after a ten story fall.

The suitcase is very airtight.
It's water and explosion-proof, too.
I'm pleased as punch about this case
Let's pack and then we are through.

I'm wearing my heavy winter clothes
Because it's real cold here,
But in that sunny southern state
It's hot, but don't you fear.

I'm putting in my summer clothes,
An outfit for each day,
Including my fashionable tennis garb.
I'm making time to play.

I'm putting my checkbook and my cash
Safely in my case.
I know I should keep some out,
But it's such a secure place.

Well, I'm ready for this business trip,
As ready as I can be.
Honey, just so nothing can go wrong
I'll keep this case with me.

Did you put my business papers
Where I told you to,
In the suitcase filing section?
If you did, then we are through.

Stewardess, thanks for the ride
And the patience you did show
When I kept my case with me
You bent the rules, I know.

THE LORD SPEAKS:

Sid, Welcome to the sunny South.
You've planned this trip out well.
By the way, I agree with you;
Your suitcase sure is swell.

But you have cause for some concern
And for an answer, don't ask Me,
For on the plane that just took off
You left your suitcase key.

The Suit

Now, family, I'm not one to brag,
But today I know I must.
I will tell you of my adventure,
If your keeping quiet I can trust.

On my lunch hour today
I had time for just one stop,
So with my checkbook I headed out
To Slipshod's silk and satin shop.

Every Easter I miss the parade,
But this year I need not pout,
For I purchased a silken suit,
And indeed I went all out.

I saw in Slipshod's window,
Yesterday afternoon,
A pair of satin boots
That simply made me swoon.

I bought those boots this very day,
Because they match the new suit of mine.
Slipshod said they were the color
Of newly foot-stomped wine.

So in a short time I'll be ready
To march right down the aisle.
Of course I'll stop at Bidwell's pew
To show him my Easter style.

Old Bidwell always leads the parade
When the Easter service is through,
But this year I'll be chosen
When my new outfit folks can view.

Family. I'm only doing this,
Because Bidwell needs to learn
That believing he must lead the parade,
Is an attitude he must spurn.

So, when I'm chosen to be first,
I hope that Bidwell will not whine,
When he sees me in my silken suit.
Which is the color of foot-stomped wine.

Now, I really like old Bidwell,
But the man has got to know;
That there's a lot more to Easter,
Than putting on a show.

So, once again, I step into the gap,
To help a misguided one find his way,
To the back of the parade line,
Where Bidwell needs to stay.

Now, If I can get the pastor to hurry up,
And let us out at noon,
We can do the parade and still make it,
To the Buffet at Greasewell's Greasy Spoon.

Tomorrow I'll go to Slipshod's,
The resizing will be through;
And I'll be the star of the parade,
When the Easter service is through.

THE LORD SPEAKS:

Sid, what about the Easter service?
Of that, you have not said a word.
Doesn't the Resurrection story
Cause your heart to be stirred?

Oh, by the way, Slipshod sold you a lemon,
In the sunshine the suit will fade.
By the time you get into church,
It will be an orange lemon shade.

However, the parade must go on,
So, Sid, just get in line.
Old Bidwell will be first again,
And at the end you will be fine.

The Kit

Hello pastor, this is Sidney,
You know, I've been inspired!
I heard the Reverend Rollie Ready,
It's said in a white suit he is attired.

Reverend Ready is really ready,
For that journey in the sky.
You know the one I'm talking about:
When to heaven we will fly.

Today he offered to one and all
"Rollie Ready's Emergency Redemption Kit."
And to help keep the cost down,
It comes in a one size fits - all fit.

It includes the "Prayerful Parachute,"
For when you are flying in the air.
And because the engines break down,
You must parachute from there.

When the parachute pops open,
Embroidered in the canopy,
Is a comforting set of verses,
That the plunger can easily see.

Also in the Redemption Kit,
Is "Reverend Rollie's Climbing Rope."
It's for when you are rock climbing,
And you realize there is no hope.

Imagine you're at two hundred feet,
The Rock above and below is sheer.
As you fall and while you're flailing,
You'll have God's Word very near.

You just reach into your kit,
And pull out the Climbing Cord,
Embroidered in the extra thin rope,
Are verses about the Lord.

Now, suppose you're in a burning building,
Up on the fifteenth floor.
You smell smoke in the hallway,
When you open up the door.

Reverend Rollie has the answer,
Right in his Redemption Kit.
It's called "Reverend Rollie's First Floor Finder,"
And it has become quite a hit.

It is a two hundred-fifty foot "Rollie Rope,"
On which, to the ground, you'll sail.
At the last moment you will bounce,
Then on to safety without fail..

Once again, the rope is embroidered,
With verses tried and true.
You can read them while you're falling,
And they will comfort you.

The Reverend Rollie Ready,
Does not have an asking price.
But, the Good Reverend Rollie,
Thinks one thousand dollars would be nice.

I think that we should order twenty,
One for each member of the Board.
Reverend Rollie says we must be ready,
When it's our time to meet the Lord.

THE LORD SPEAKS:

Sid, I know you'll have a problem,
If the twenty thousand dollar check is sent.
It will be taken by Reverend Ready,
And by him it will be spent.

You listened to Reverend Rollie via radio,
He pastors a church of one.
Not counting his wife Bertwilla,
And his most rebellious son.

I've seen his Ordination papers,
Though they all look real nice,
The man who signed the papers,
Is being chased by cops from vice.

As well, I checked my calculator
And a fifteen story fall,
Is forty feet shorter than the "Rollie Rope,"
And Sid, that is not all.

The parachute has no ripcord,
And who will hold the Climbing Rope?"
In fact, the "Redemption Kit,"
Assures you'll have no hope.

Sid, you almost got sucked in,
By a money hungry scheme.
Sidney, next time, take a closer look,
Things are not always as they seem!

The Bible

Here I am at the Bible Book Store,
My old Bible I must replace.
Because this store focuses on Bibles,
They take up most of the space.

This is an incredible Bible buffet,
So I've asked God to see me through.
I know he'll send me some assistance,
The salesperson will know what to do.

Honey, I'm home from my adventure,
My purchase has been made.
Now, don't get all excited,
About the price I've paid.

This Bible provides the answer,
To any question you may ask.
After I take the "Use This Bible" seminar,
I'll be up to the task.

My new Bible has four versions,
Set neatly side by side.
It resolves the problem,
Of, when the meaning seems to hide.

We know how important the Bible is,
As we live from day to day.
Now, I've got all the answers,
To help us along the way.

The first version is the regular one,
That I received long ago.
I can remember when I won it,
At the youth fellowship talent show.

It will serve as my launch point,
When I have time to read.
The other three versions,
Focus on a special need.

The "Help You Get Up In The Morning" version,
Is located in column two.
Every word that has to do with getting up,
Is underlined in blue.

The "Art Of Responsible Eating" version,
Can be found in column three.
Each time food is mentioned,
Those words, in green, I see.

The "Help Your Pastor When He's Stuck
For A Word" version
Comprises column number four,
Each word has an alternate,
That you can share with him at the door.

Well, here it is! The solution,
To every problem that is mine.
If I use this wisely and keep it in it's box,
I know all will be just fine.

By the way, on the back cover,
Of this purchase I just made,
Is a battery operated calculator,
That justifies the price I paid.

It includes an alarm clock feature,
Along with a diet plan,
As well, a bible word pronouncer,
To help the pastor when I can.

THE LORD SPEAKS:

Sid, you're quick to get on board,
When something new comes your way.
I may just be old-fashioned,
But with the original one I'll stay.

You only need the regular one,
In the translation of your choice.
As you read it to find an answer,
You will hear my voice.

By the way, Sid, the calculator,
That you are so eager to try,
Has a non-replaceable dead battery,
So another bible you must buy.

Printed in the United States
34161LVS00002BA/262-309